D.I.Y. MAKE IT HAPPEN

BAND

VIRGINIA LOH-HAGAN

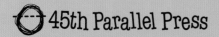 45th Parallel Press

Published in the United States of America by Cherry Lake Publishing
Ann Arbor, Michigan
www.cherrylakepublishing.com

Reading Adviser: Marla Conn, ReadAbility, Inc.
Book Designer: Felicia Macheske

Photo Credits: © Andresr/Shutterstock.com, cover, 1; © fotum/Shutterstock.com, 3; © Ververidis Vasilis/Shutterstock.com, 5; © cosma/Shutterstock.com, 7; © leungchopan/Shutterstock.com, 9; © by_nicholas/iStock, 11; © trekandshoot/Shutterstock.com, 14; © Jaimie Duplass/Shutterstock.com, 15; © April Cat/Shutterstock.com, 17; © Fuse/Thinkstock, 18; © Tarzhanova/Shutterstock.com, 19, 31; © Nicole Weiss/Shutterstock.com, 20; © Hedzun Vasyl/Shutterstock.com, 21; © wavebreakmedia/Shutterstock.com, 23; © hartcreations/iStock, 25; © Thomas Spayth/Shutterstock.com, 27, 30; © Syda Productions/Shutterstock.com, 28; © wavebreakmedia/Shutterstock.com, back cover; © Dora Zett/Shutterstock.com, back cover

Graphic Elements: © pashabo/Shutterstock.com, 6, back cover; © axako/Shutterstock.com, 7; © IreneArt/Shutterstock.com, 4, 8; © bokasin/Shutterstock.com, 11, 19; © Belausava Volha/Shutterstock.com, 12, 20; © Nik Merkulov/Shutterstock.com, 13; © Ya Tshey/Shutterstock.com, 16, 27; © kubais/Shutterstock.com, 17; © Sasha Nazim/Shutterstock.com, 15, 24; © topform/Shutterstock.com, 21, 22, back cover; © Ursa Major/Shutterstock.com, 23, 28; © Infomages/Shutterstock.com, 26; © Art'nLera/Shutterstock.com, back cover

45th Parallel Press is an imprint of Cherry Lake Publishing.

Library of Congress Cataloging-in-Publication Data

Loh-Hagan, Virginia.
 Band / by Virginia Loh-Hagan.
   pages cm. — (D.I.Y. make it happen)
 Includes bibliographical references and index.
 ISBN 978-1-63470-498-4 (hardcover) — ISBN 978-1-63470-558-5 (pdf) — ISBN 978-1-63470-618-6 (pbk.) —
ISBN 978-1-63470-678-0 (ebook)
 1. Musical groups—Vocational guidance—Juvenile literature. I. Title.
 ML3795.L6 2016
 784.023—dc23
                              2015026845

Cherry Lake Publishing would like to acknowledge the work of The Partnership for 21st Century Skills.
Please visit *www.p21.org* for more information.

Printed in the United States of America
Corporate Graphics Inc.

ABOUT THE AUTHOR

Dr. Virginia Loh-Hagan is an author, university professor, former classroom teacher, and curriculum designer. She has three pianos, two guitars, and one violin. She would love to be in a band. But she's scared of performing in public. She lives in San Diego with her very tall husband and very naughty dogs. To learn more about her, visit www.virginialoh.com.

TABLE OF CONTENTS

CHAPTER ONE

WHAT DOES IT MEAN TO START A BAND?

Do you love singing songs? Do you love playing instruments? Do you love performing? Then starting a band is the right project for you!

Bands are musical groups. They work together. They make music. There are all types of bands. Rock bands are one type. They have a lead singer. They have guitar players. They have a drummer. They have a keyboard player.

Band members love music. They perform at **gigs**. Gigs are shows or concerts. They play a **set**. A set is a song list. They play for an **audience**. Audience refers to people. These people watch shows.

Go see some live shows.
Meet band members.

KNOW THE LINGO

A cappella: singing without instruments

Bridge: musical connection between the last verse and chorus

Chops: good music skills

Encore: the audience wanting the band to perform more songs

Groupie: a very devoted fan

Hook: a catchy melody that sticks in the listener's mind

Jam session: a spontaneous musical performance

Lick: a bit of music that doesn't repeat

Light show: using lighting effects during a show

Merch: short for merchandise; promotional materials

On tour: playing at different places

Opening act: a band that warms up the crowd before the main band performs

Payola: bribing disc jockeys to play songs on the radio

Riff: a recognizable part of a song

Sell-out crowd: audience in a sold-out show

Vamp: a repeated pattern that fills time before the main melody

Start a band whenever you want! Bands perform all year long.

Bands perform at different events. They perform at parties. They perform at weddings. They perform in restaurants. Some bands make money. Some perform for **exposure**. Exposure means getting attention. Bands want people to know them. They play to get more gigs. Some want to be famous. Some play for fun.

You'll have fun starting your own band. You'll play songs you love. You'll play with friends. You'll meet lots of people.

Split money equally among all band members.

CHAPTER TWO

WHAT DO YOU NEED TO START A BAND?

Think about what type of band you want.

➡ Decide the music you want to play. There are many types. Some examples are rock, rap, and punk. The music will determine the instruments you need. (Punk music needs guitar players. It needs a drummer. It needs a singer.)

➡ Decide your goals. Do you want to play in private? Do you want to play in public? Do you want a job in the music business? Do you play as a hobby? Do you want to make money?

➡ Decide your songs. Will you sing **cover** songs? These are songs written and sung by other musicians. Will you write your own songs? These are **original** songs. Or you could sing both song types.

Listen to different types of music. Many musicians combine types.

Choose band members. This is an important decision. You'll spend lots of time together. You want to get along.

➡ Find musicians. Ask friends. Put up posters at school. Host **auditions**. These are tryouts. Pick the right people. Bands usually have four to five people.

➡ Decide who will be the lead singer.

➡ Decide who will play instruments.

➡ Get a band manager. This person takes care of money. This person sets up gigs. This person **promotes** you. Promoting is letting others know about you.

➡ Get a **roadie**. Roadies help set up band gear. They also help put it away. They do this before and after gigs.

Consider having band members sign a contract.

Decide a band name. This is how people will know you. Everyone should agree on the name.

➡ Brainstorm a list of names. You have lots of choices. Band names can be real things. They can be made up. They can be anything.

➡ Narrow down your list. Try combining ideas.

➡ Choose your favorite name.

➡ Create a **logo**. A logo is a picture.

Decide your band look.

➡ Decide what you want to wear. Your clothes should match the music. Some bands wear costumes.

➡ Decide your makeup. Some band members put black lines around their eyes. Some cover their faces.

➡ Decide your hairstyles.

Try out your band name. Tell other people. Get their opinions.

TRY THIS!

All bands want to get their music heard. Most bands have fans. Fans follow bands to their shows. Host a "Battle of the Bands"! Get several bands and their fans in one place. More people will hear you play. You'll also enjoy the competition.

You'll need: promotional materials, four to seven bands, prizes, judges, an announcer

Steps

1 **Find a place to perform.**

2 **Determine a date. A Saturday night would be best.**

3 **Invite several bands to play and compete.**

4 **Create and send out posters and flyers. Tell everybody about it!**

5 **Host a night of live music.**

6 **Get an announcer to introduce each band.**

7 **Have each band play three to five songs.**

8 **Have a committee of judges choose winners. The judges should not be loyal to any one band.**

9 **Hand out prizes.**

Bands have a lot of gear.

➡ You can buy, rent, or borrow instruments. Get carrying cases.

➡ **Amplifiers** make instruments louder. They're hooked to instruments. They send sounds to **speakers**.

➡ Speakers are like sound boxes. They're hooked to amplifiers. They're hooked to **microphones**.

➡ **Microphones are used by singers. They make singers' voices louder.**

➡ **Microphone stands hold microphones. They stay in one place.**

➡ **Electric cords are needed. They're used to plug in equipment.**

➡ **Recording gear lets you record your music.**

Bring extra gear to gigs.
Things break. Things get lost.

CHAPTER THREE

HOW DO YOU SET UP A BAND?

Practice a lot. There are two types of practice.

➡ **Solo practice is by yourself. Practice your instrument. Practice your songs.**

➡ **Band practice is with the band. You combine your skills. You arrange music.**

Get a place for band rehearsals. Rehearsals are band practice sessions.

➡ **Use available space. Use basements or garages. Use a room at school.**

➡ **Respect your neighbors. Don't practice late at night. Don't practice more than a couple of hours a day.**

➡ **Set levels. Don't practice too loudly. Protect your ears.**

DANIEL KOHN

Daniel Kohn writes and speaks about the music business. He was also in bands. By age 13, he toured with Sonic Youth. At age 15, his band signed a record deal. By age 16, they toured around the world. He played with Foo Fighters, Beck, and others. He advises networking and meeting people. He said, "Make sure you are always carrying a ton of your CDs in your backpack wherever you go. And make sure that your band is at the front of nearly every single conversation you have with anyone remotely involved in the music world. ... The other benefit of networking like crazy is that when you do get gigs, you've slowly built up a list of people to bring along to the show. And hopefully some of them will know your tunes because you gave them a CD to listen to."

Don't waste band practice time learning your individual part.

Create a regular schedule. Daily practice
is best.

➡ **Assign someone to be in charge.**

➡ **Warm up. Practice songs that aren't in your set.
Practice songs you know.**

➡ **Rehearse your set list. Pick several songs to
master.**

Decide your band's songs.

➡ **Write your own songs.**

➡ **Choose cover songs. Add your own sound. Most bands start by playing cover songs. People like hearing songs they know.**

Make a demo. It's a recording. It's a demonstration of your band's sound. It's a way to promote your band.

➡ **Include two or three songs.**

➡ **Include original music.**

➡ **Choose your best songs.**

➡ **Record in your home studio.**

➡ **Keep the masters. These are the first recordings of songs. Copies are made from masters.**

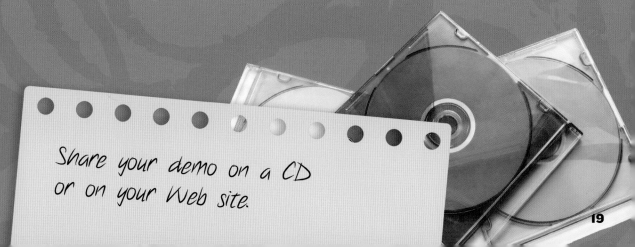

Share your demo on a CD or on your Web site.

Look online or in newspapers
to find gigs.

Set up your gigs. A band manager can take care of this. But everyone should help.

➡ **Find local places that host live music. This includes restaurants and coffee shops. Introduce yourself to the owners. Give them a demo.**

➡ **Make friends with other local bands. Offer to open for them. Sing before they sing. Warm up the crowd.**

➡ **Enter contests. This includes your school's talent show.**

➡ **Play at house parties. Play at fairs. Play anywhere! Get exposure.**

➡ **Create your own show. Choose a night. Choose a place. Invite all your friends. Play your music.**

To be a popular band, you need to promote yourself. This is part of the band manager's job. But everyone should help.

➡ **Create a Web site. Share pictures. Share information. Share a schedule of gigs.**

➡ **Use social media. Post videos of rehearsals. Post videos of performances. Share funny stories. Share news.**

➡ **Create a press kit. Include your demo. Include information. Include nice comments from fans. Send it to people who can get you gigs.**

➡ **Create merchandise. These are things you can sell or give away. Examples are shirts, hats, and posters.**

➡ **Ask a fan to start a fan club.**

Put press kit items in
a nice folder.

CHAPTER FOUR

HOW DO YOU RUN A BAND AT A GIG?

You've got a band. You've rehearsed. You've promoted the band. You've got a gig. You're ready for the big night!
Do several things before you perform.

➡ Check out the place. Do this a couple of days before. Check out their equipment.

➡ Print the set list in large letters. This is so band members can read it. Give everybody a copy. Place it on the floor. Place it by the instruments.

➡ Be early.

➡ **Load in**. This means set up your instruments. Set up your gear. Figure out your places onstage.

➡ Do a **sound check**. This means check your gear. Make sure everything is working. You can also practice. Check out how you sound. Every room makes different sounds.

➡ **Assign someone to film your performance.**

Make sure to use the bathroom before you perform!

QUICK TIPS

- To raise money, try crowdsourcing. Use the Internet to raise funds. Ask people to donate money for your band. People donate online.

- During live shows, you'll make mistakes. Play through it. Don't announce your mistakes. Don't say you're sorry.

- People won't notice 90 percent of your musical mistakes. But they notice equipment problems. Learn and know about your gear.

- During rehearsals, go over mistakes. Don't play through. Start back at the beginning.

- Rewrite songs. Play with different moods or tempos. Tempo is speed. Change genre. Turn a rap song into a ballad. This is a great exercise. It helps you become a better musician.

- Ask someone to record silly things that happen during rehearsals. Share them on social media.

- Practice a lot. Before the Beatles became a hit, they played more than 1,200 concerts. They played nonstop. They played eight hours a night. They played seven nights a week. They were forced to get better.

Do several things when you're onstage.

➡ **Introduce your band name.**

➡ **Perform your set list.**

➡ **Stay on beat. Some people perform faster onstage. They're nervous. Stay focused.**

➡ **Stay in the time limit. Other bands may play after you. Don't go over your given time.**

➡ **Look at the crowd. Maintain eye contact. Your fans are important.**

➡ **Engage people between songs. Avoid dead air. Dead air is silence. Practice song banter. Talk to each other between songs. Talk to the audience.**

➡ **Have fun! Playing in a band is hard work. But it's also cool!**

Practice song banter during rehearsals as well.

Promote yourself on and
off stage.

Do several things after you perform.

➡ **Thank everyone for coming. Thank your hosts.**

➡ **Introduce band members and their instruments.**

➡ **Other bands may be performing. Say good things about them.**

➡ **Clean your area. Pack up your stuff. Wipe things down. Most band members get sweaty.**

➡ **If it's a paying gig, collect money. The band manager can do this.**

➡ **Post your performance video online.**

➡ **Talk to your band members. Discuss what went well. Discuss what you could do better.**

Hang out with your fans.

➡ **Give away or sell merchandise.**

➡ **Ask people to follow you on social media.**

➡ **Tell them about your upcoming gigs!**

D.I.Y. EXAMPLE!

STEPS	EXAMPLES
Band type	An all-girl band that plays catchy popular songs with a rock and country feel
Band members	➤ I will play piano or keyboard. ➤ My sister will be lead singer. ➤ My friends will play fiddle, guitar, and drums. ➤ My little sister and brother will be roadies. ➤ My cousin will be band manager.
Band name	Yellow Sandwiches
Band look	Yellow dresses, cowboy boots, punk hair

STEPS	EXAMPLES
Plan for rehearsals	• Where: My basement • When: Every day after school for one hour and on Saturday for two hours
Get a gig	School talent show
Set list/demo songs	• Cover song: "Roar" by Katy Perry • Original song: "Gray Skies" • Original song: "Dotted Lines"
Promotional plan	• Send out press kit with demo and business cards to local restaurants and coffee shop owners. • Host a contest for people to design our logo and band poster. • Give out T-shirts and wristbands with our logo to the first 50 people who sign up for our online mailing list.

GLOSSARY

amplifiers (AM-plih-fye-urz) devices that make electronic instruments louder; they send sounds to speakers

audience (AW-dee-uhns) people who see a show

auditions (aw-DISH-uhnz) tryouts

cover (KUHV-ur) songs that have been written or sung by other musicians

dead air (DED AIR) silence

demo (DEM-oh) a recording that demonstrates a band's sound

exposure (ik-SPOH-zhur) getting attention, getting noticed

gigs (GIGZ) shows or concerts

load in (LOHD IN) set up instruments and equipment before a gig

logo (LOH-goh) a picture or image used to represent a group

masters (MAS-turz) first recordings of songs, used to make copies

merchandise (MUR-chun-dise) things you can give away or sell

microphones (MYE-kruh-fonez) devices that singers sing into and that make voices louder

original (uh-RIJ-uh-nuhl) new songs written by you

press kit (PRES KIT) a packet of information to give to promoters

promotes (pruh-MOTES) lets others know about your band

rehearsals (rih-HURS-uhlz) band practice sessions

roadie (ROHD-ee) a person who sets up and tears down band equipment

set (SET) a list of songs

solo (SOH-loh) alone

song banter (SAWNG BAN-tur) talking between songs to avoid dead air

sound check (SOUND CHEK) checking equipment and sound before a gig

speakers (SPEEK-erz) sound boxes, hooked to amplifiers and microphones

studio (STOO-dee-oh) a special place to record music; it has recording equipment

INDEX

LEARN MORE

BOOKS

5 Seconds of Summer. *Hey, Let's Make a Band! The Official 5SOS Book.* New York: HarperCollins, 2014.

Harmon, Daniel E. *How to Start Your Own Band.* New York: Rosen Central, 2012.

WEB SITES

eHow—"How to Start a Band": www.ehow.com/how_2248584_start-band.html

WikiHow—"How to Make Your Own Hit Band": www.wikihow.com/Make-Your-Own-Hit-Band-(Kids)